The Death of a Veteran

Tales from the Smoke House

By

Franklin P Smith

copyright Aug 2016

Authors Notes

This tale is what happens happen when I went to the Atlanta Veterans Hospital. The portions written in the font of 'hand writing' is what happen to me. I did nothing to ask for this kind of treatment.

The later portion of what happen to the person who is a fictional character does happen because the actions when a person is not given help and continually put off with their 'Protocol' approach to saving money and treatment of veterans.

People will say, "You had this just happen to you." My response is this kind of action by the Veterans Administration has been documented time and time.

No Veteran has access to the power brokers in Washington D. C.. There is always the 'patient advocate ' -they are big joke - (I have done this many times and results is zero and probably the same result from other conner people and the patient wanting help).

In a nut shell, the Atlanta Veterans Hospital did nothing to get rid of my pain, help me exist. I had to all of it. The only thing that they did was to give me surgery on my eyes. This was afterwards when I was in Navy, I was transfer out of my job because I wrote my congressman wanting someone to fix my eye problem.

This happens.

I would like to know - what did I do to deserve this kind of abuse and lack of care from the personnel from Veterans Administration.

Franklin P Smith

"Hey, are you the writer?" a voice rang out deep in the rack of paper books.

Suddenly, a medium size man appear between the two book racks in front of the semi-circle where the old men sat in the afternoon solving all the worlds' problems and predicting what would happen if this or that would happen. At present, sitting in the semi-circle was Pat, the resident writer and story teller.

"I guess, you are looking for me," Pat responded looking directly at this man. The man was 5-11 and medium built. Pat notice, the man, was carrying a stack of loose yellow pad pages in his right hand. Pat wondered what this person was up too. Harry had told me a young man carrying a bundle of yellow pad pages had asked him two days in a row about the 'writer.'

Good morning," Pat exclaim in a loud voice but not too loud. "What brings you out so early. The old men don't come in until around one," Pat said pausing briefly. "They do put on a show."

"I'm here to see you," the man replied. "I hear about you since I move to town.

I moved here about three months ago. I'm working at the bakery as a programmer.

Can I sit and tell you a story of sorts." the man said approaching one of the bamboo chairs.

"Well, I want to tell you really about this guy, I lived next too where I use to live….He was a unique person," the man paused speaking briefly.

"He killed himself," the man said as he sat down in a bamboo chair directly across from Pat.

There was a dead silence between the two men.

The stranger spoke in a distinct manner. "My name is Ted.

Anyway, I was living next to this guy. His name was Fred and around 65 years old. I had been living next to him for several years but never really took an interest in the guy. One day, when I return home from work, he pulling up in a taxi. The taxi driver brought a case of bourbon into his place. As I pass them, he hollered out, "Come over for a drink after you get settled in," Well, I never turn down free drinks," Ted stop talking catching his breath and placing the stack of the yellow pad papers on the bamboo chair next to him. The man acted really tense with his movements.

"You sound kind parched," Pat said. "You see the red Coke cooler over there. Go over there and get you something to drink and above the cooler, there is a rack full of moon pies. You ever had an orange crush drink and a moon pie?"

4

"No," Ted replied.

"Well, here is your chance and you'll never be the same," Pat said as Ted got up an secured a moon pie and an orange drink.

"Man, this taste great,' Ted replied after he took two bites from the moon pie and chased it with the Orange drink.

"As, I was saying. Fred had invited me over for drinks. I was totally shocked as I enter his apartment. In the middle of the living was a dining room table. With two chairs around the table with each chair across the table. What took me was what was on the table. There were about five fifth liquor bottles with on half full of bourbon. With in the mist of the bottles, there were numerous pill bottles and pills on the table indistinctly spread on the table top. In the front of one chair was a large revolver. I had never seen such a big gun.

Fred noticed that I was staring at the weapon. "Oh, that's my play toy for my evenings,' Fred remark.

"I invited you for a drink," Fred said in a pragmatic tone. "I got to get you a glass," disappearing from the living room.

In returning Fred when over to the table and open the case of liquor. "This not the best stuff but it works. A friend told me once, "You only taste the first glass even you get the real good stuff. Your taste buds become num after the first touch of the alcohol. The only thing that matters in the first half hour is its bite. I knew a moonshiner once that make stuff that would slip in your mouth down to your stomach, and you would not know its kick until it hit your guts. Then your world would go upside down. But, I prefer the stuff that has a bite to it," Fred said retrieving a bottle from the case.

"Why?" I ask.

"Well, I've such a wonderful life, I guess the bigger bite will erase all those crappy moments," Fred said while he pour a half glass for me and a full glass for himself. Fred quickly made the liquid in his glass disappear and immediately pour himself another full glass.

I just sip on my glass as surveyed the living room. There was beautiful painted pictures neck to neck on each wall space. I had never seen such powerful paintings. This guy was good at what he did!

"I see you like my work," Fred said as he pour himself another full glass of liquor. "That's I do or should say did."

"I don't do that anymore," Fred said after he drank his third drink within ten minutes.

"You must have been thirsty," I said.

"Well, you might say, 'It's my medicine.'" Fred said pouring the fourth drink. "Heck, some months I go through two cases."

"I've got to go," I told him. "I've got to go to work tomorrow."

"Drop by Saturday; we can watch football. I got all those channels most people don't have," Fred said putting his hand on my shoulder. "We can order pizza, too."

I left and I had no intention of going back, but Saturday I was doing laundry and I had really nothing to do when Fred knock on the door.

"You coming over?' Fred said. "I have a large pizza with the stuff on it. I did put those fish on there. I ate those things once, and it was the most disgusting thing that I have ever eaten.'

"I guess the 'die' was cast between us. Every Saturday and Sunday both of us would get plastered. I glad when the Super Bowl was over. After every weekend, I was wondering if my liver or kidneys could survive all the alcohol, I had consumed. About mid-week, I would shake my head of how this guy could drink the way seven days of the week but he did.

During our drinking he would revel a little about his past and how his money was supplied. He was an average paint but in his travels, he found an art gallery for the 'rich.' I mean rich. These folks thought nothing of dropping thousands for a painting.

I guess, it only took Fred a couple of years hitting up those kind of folks, and he was set for life. Heck, he had no wife, kids, no car or brothers or sisters. His folks had died years ago, and I guess this was his 'seed' money in finding his nitch in the art world. His rent was 600 a month, and the only major expense was his booze that bought every month.

I some of us have it made.

Something happen right before the Super Bowl. He started not to talk and drink more - if he could, but he did. He was buying an extra case a week.

One evening, I had invited him over to cook out. He came. I was surprised because I had ask him numerous times before. He came bring three bottles of bourbon and left with less than a half a bottle. I only drank a half a bottle; he drank the rest.

After we had eaten, his behavior suddenly change to a serious number.

"I've got to tell you something," he told point in a serious tone. I was taken his abrupt sober direction in his behavior.

"I guess, you wonder about my drinking," he said as I sat down across from him. "I haven't anything to live for." I didn't say a word. I didn't what to say or how to handle a person with kind of attitude.

"I have my toy," he said in a quiet tone and very audible sound. "I play with it every time - maybe twice."

"They have said my paints will pass the test of time, but I just throw the paint on the canvas. I have over 50,000 for one painting. I can't see that but that what they want to pay.

I've really sick and in pain all my life. My parents died early in my life. I join the Navy before I got drafted for Vietnam. If it had been a normal draft but they were wanting bodies to go to kill Charlie, I would have never pass the physical, but I had no control over my destiny.

After the Navy, I went to art school on the GI Bill. I got married, and she die suddenly in a car accident. I got pile money from that because it was the other guy's fault," Fred was silent. The silence continue for the longest time. I thought I had to say something for this guy to feel better but my mind was swimming with the booze, and I had never been caught between a rock and a hard place where you had to help someone that wanted to end it all. I knew the safest thing was to keep my mouth shut. I did this.

"I really miss having and being with a woman. I loved her making love to me. There is nothing in the world like that," Fred was silent again.

"Then the pain came. I had gone to an eye doctor. He told me that I had an eye infection. He gave me drops to kill the infection. It cure the infection but suddenly I realize I had been in pain all my life. I had been going to the VA for help with my sinus infections but they had done hardly anything for me.

This is when the real hell came into play," Fred suddenly stop speaking.

"I got to go home!!" Fred said loudly. "I got to go home!!"

I didn't want him to go, but this was his privilege and surely had no intervention skills solve his problem.

Suddenly, my mouth open and said this, "Why don't you write about your pain and what you went through. It might help."

"I've got to go now!!!!" Fred as he got up and walk through my front door.

"I come over after work to see about you," I said. I don't know if he heard me.

I went over the next evening. We drank a little together. The only different with his table was several pieces of yellow table paper.

We watch the Super Bowl, and both of us got real drunk. After that I would go over to his place once during the week and have him over to cook out every other week end," Ted said in a slow, methodical manner and was quiet.

Pat knew this - this was his story, and everyone has their own cadence to tell their story.

"You know he was different after the first cook out," Ted said in dramatic way.

"Every time, I went over to his place, he had his toy on the table. I wondered when the odds would catch up with Fred.

Well, it did about a two from then.

It was about ten at night that I heard the loud noise. I knew instinctively what happen. He had finally had gotten what he wanted - relieve from his pain and the rejection had experience in seeking help for his pain.

I went over there immediately. I open the door...he never lock his doors.

I saw his upper portion of his body slump over on the table. What I saw wanted me to throw-up. His head was half blown off. Blood was everywhere. The more I walk into the room more my stomach wanted to expel what I had eaten for supper.

Standing next to the table, I look at the table. There four empty liquor bottles with one with one-third of the brown liquor left in the bottle. There were yellow sheets from a writing pad spread over the table. There several empty bottles of pill bottles and pills spill spread out on top of the yellow sheets.

7

I don't why, but I pick up most of these sheets and folded them up and after roll them up I place them in my back pocket. I probably thought Fred had put some real personal stuff on these papers that didn't need to be read. Well, I was half right.

You have all them. I read about half of them. They made me sick and at the same time angry. Most of what I read was how the VA had mess with him and just plainly put him off for years. I had heard stories from friends about their friends and how they would be treated, but I thought from the news reports that the problem with these people had been fix.

I was wrong!" Ted said as he got from the bamboo chair.

"Where is the restroom? I have to go." Ted said.

"It's in the back just before you go out the backdoor...on the right." Pat replied to the man's request. "I'll do it while you're gone."

Pat pick up the stack of yellow sheets as Ted disappear into the back.

I have to get these thoughts out of my head of what has happened to me.

When did it start?

I was serving in the US Navy beating the draft. I could have been drafted and had a red plus sign on my back wading through the rice paddings of Southeast Asia.

I was a Personnel-man third class serving my last year of a four-year enlistment. I was seriously thinking of making the Navy my career. However, during the later part of the second year, I found myself unable to pass the typing requirements to be qualified to take the second class exam., I had notice that I had missing things as entered data into the enlisted service records. I complain to my chief in the Personnel Office and one day I realized something was wrong with my eyes - I was swapping eyes while I was typing. I went to my Chief and told him what was happening. He did not pay attention to me. I went to sick bay but they just pass my complain over as just one of those things. I wrote my Senator and with a month of writing this letter, I was transfer into a non-personnel role in another division and help build the first store on the USS Roosevelt. I still complain but nothing was done. While on the shake-down curse for the Roosevelt a notice was given to enlisted personnel for an early out. From the rejection from the personnel and the medical people on the Roosevelt, I knew the Navy was not for me. What I did realize then that this attitude would follow me the rest of my life in seeking help from the Veterans Administration.

I had other medical problems, but when I went to sick call, the medic would always put me off with some excuse in not treating me.

I was surprised when I went to the Atlanta VA that they diagnosis me with muscle problems with my eyes. The ENT doctor informed me that I would lean my head a certain way where I would see with both eyes, or I would focus with the left or the right eye. They did surgery and decreased the angle where I could wear glass with prisms in my eyes.

I was having sinuses infections and decided to let the Atlanta VA handle this problem since they had done a decent job with my eyes.

The infections came with an unbelievable pain and at times was unbearable to endure.

I was given antibiotics, but the pain was still there. My Physician Assistant on one visit gave me a 1,000 aspirin. However, the pain increased and the infection still was giving me pain that I could barely bare. Walking out with Brennan, the PA, I ask him to point blankly what about my pain?": He replied, "I gave you a 1,000 aspirin." I knew at that moment the road to get help with the VA Hospital would be a dead end. With this pain my blood pressure increase to the point the PA gave me blood pressure meds. The high blood pressure was due to the pain that was caused by the pain that I endured.

I work at this time as a convention worker. With my health insurance, I went outside the VA to obtain surgery to see if I could get rid of the pain that I was enduring. The VA did not want to do anything about the pain and infections that I was enduring.

Yet, the infections and the pain still was there. I was bleeding on top of everything but still the PA would not do anything to help me.

At this time I was in the Master's program to be a teacher at a local University.

I was focusing on my studies, working part-time, taking care of my two children. These were my goals to accomplish.

Suddenly, the PA sent me to the ENT Department. By this time the pain was increasing and I was having stroke-like symptoms for the next 12 years.

After losing my wife - the load was unbelievable - raising two children, making a living, and going to school. My goal was to function and earn money where I could survive.

I still when to the ENT doctors. They would order Cat Scans and MRI's, but they would tell that they could not find the infection or infections. I endured these infections until I got Medicare. Obtain Medicare I went to an outside ENT person. After the infection would not go away, the doctor printed out the Cat Scan and found the infection. The doctors at the VA never printed out the Cat Scans out. During this period when I saw these doctors at the VA I went to the doctor in charge of the Clinics. He told me that the VA could not afford to send me outside the VA for a private doctor to see me so I went back to the same doctors who would not take the second step in printing out the MRI's or Cat Scans.

I transfer to the Stockbridge clinic when the clinic opened up. I live across the interstate highway from the clinic. I went to register at the Clinic. I was told that I could not because I did not get an invitation. The place had been open only two weeks and really no one was coming to the clinic. I was persistent, and the personnel finally accepted me.

However, treatment at the clinic was terrible. The waiting period was from two hours to sis hours, and this was when a person had an appointment. The treatment from the doctors was just as worse as the doctors at the ENT department at the main VA Hospital. At times, I had to beg for antibiotic for my sinuses infection. On one occasion, I had to contact a congressman to get some antibiotics for infections. I was put in the hospital that is located next to this clinic for an irregular heart beat. This is where the hospital discovered that I had been over-dosed with blood pressure, and I was anemic. On getting out of the hospital, I walk to the clinic. I told them about me being anemic. They did nothing. I went home, and I was weak that I could not barely wash my dirty dishes. It took me two months to get the B-12 shots that I needed. My doctor at the time want to take another month for the stool cards to tell her that I was anemic. She had already done the blood work that prove this fact.

On one of the Cat Scans, it show that I had a cyst in my upper gum. I went to dental. There were two sessions of pulling my upper teeth. After both surgeries, the dentist did not give me any antibiotics. This is not to mention these dentists leaving broken pieces of teeth in my upper gum. They did call four months later telling me that they heard that I had pieces of broken teeth in my gum.

This is not to mention I was visiting the eye clinic and told the doctor about the pain in my left cheek. He told me, "You have a tear duct stop up." He took a long needle and could not find the tear duct. The next day my upper bridge fell down. It took dental two years to get me another bridge and then it did not fit.

On one occasion, seeing the doctor for a physical, I said 'Damn' twice and the doctor call the VA Police on me to throw me out of the clinic.

Pat stop reading. He look at Ted. Ted had placid look on his face. His skin had turn a light white. The man had read what he was reading. These words had penetrated this man's soul and his soul was troubled. Pat understood. Ted had probably the same feelings that he was experiencing. How could these people treat this man In such a manner?

I cannot believe that these people still drop the ball or do they do it just put me in a box where I will kill myself. At times, I do think of it, and I guess this is why I play with my toy at least once during the evening if I am alone.

Where did all this crap start this time?

Oh, yes. It was the doctor from the Stockbridge Clinic and my crack teeth. I wrote the Chief of Staff - Bowers - about the doctor transferring me to a Decatur clinic without my knowledge. I had been told this by the doctor that manages the medication for the patient at the clinic. I then got a call late one afternoon asking me to call back. I did, but she did not call me back. I call the assistant to Bowers she went into the computer and found that I had not been transferred or put into for a transfer. I call the nurse at the Stockbridge Clinic. She told me that the transfer was in the process stage.

I understood why this doctor wanted to get rid of me. I had reported her about the way she did not to treatment. My first encounter was when my sugar was 500. She sent me to the near by hospital to fix this but she did not want too at the time hear anything else from me about what I was concern with. She just walk out of the room. Several months later, I was in for a nurse visit for some reason. I was upset because of several other major incidents that had occurred about four prior. I ask about my bouncing blood pressure. The nurse left to see the doctor to ask her about my blood pressure. She came back and told me-"Go to Kaiser." I was really upset then. The doctor did not want to care for me. The same old crap happening. The cops came - not a social worker or a mental health professional to help me. I was escorted out my the police. I remember those memories of wanting to confront Brennan about the 1,000 aspirin and once a this clinic when another doctor call two VA police after I said 'Damn' twice.. This was said in a low voice. At the time, I told the police I was not being ugly. I was told that I was being ugly and dis eruptive. They stood at the door when I got my yearly physical.

The other issue that I wrote the Chief of Staff was about my teeth. One of the crack tooth had broken off and was bad, and the infection had gone to the next tooth.

After a week, I get this call from this social therapist. She was concern about me. Big Joke! But the reason she call was that I had Bowers to call me after a week. HE NEVER DID!!! I told this person two hours of the HELL that the personnel at the Atlanta had put me through. She had told me before we ended the call-"I'm really concern about you, and I will call you tomorrow." SHE NEVER DID.

So I sent the President and email.

The flood gates broke open.

I got the phone calls. I got one from dental telling me that I was not qualified for my tooth to be pull. They sent me a list which over three-fourths were out of business just like the social worker assign me. The other quarter, I had to wait three months or more or pay money. The other phone calls were from the Crisis Center and mental health personnel. I do not know why! Granted, I had mentioned that I would jump out of the first-floor window many months because I was so frustrated at the 'non-care' from the ENT people and the VA personnel. When I ask for help in filing for my claim after they ask what they could do they hung up.

What is interesting is that from my comment about the first-floor window, I was taken into the shrink ward but let go after the Doctor shrink talk to me? I believe that he realized what the VA had and was doing to me. He ask me to see a therapist. I went. What a big joke. She left for another job after five or four visits. Her supervisor told me "It will be six months or more before we get another person for me." I ask her help in filing data about me for my pending claim. She did not say anything. Another slap in the face.

I call the Directors office and talk to the assistant to the Chief of Staff. She inform me that she could not talk to me because she had a deadline to finish the congressional that I started by the end of the day. Well, it has been nearly a month. I only got a letter stating that 'I' file the wrong forms for the claim that was denied. I follow directors by the social worker to see a certain DAV representative. I did not file any forms. Should have done this person job and cross that boundary in telling this person how to do her job.

I call the Directors a week later, and I was told that they could not or would not talk to me because they were still working on the missteps by their personnel.

I was promised by the Chief of Staff my teeth would be fix. To be fix since I will have only seven crack teeth on the bottom.will be major teeth replacement.

I made another ENT appointment. Guess who I saw? Brennan, who now is their man person in the ENT department. Here was my opportunity to confront him about the aspirin. I did and nicely believe it or not. I told him about my low B-1 and he did give me a multi-vitamin. I told him about my bleeding in my body — he made no comment. Oh, his reply to my question about the aspirin. He responded-"I only did 'protocol'. In others, if a person has constant major pain and infections, you just give him a 1,000 aspirin. At the closure of my exam, Brennan told me that I was going to have a Cat Scan or something — this never happen and I would see a 'real' doctor from Emory. I waited two months or more. I type up the events of my bleeding from my head after the Kaiser doctors gave me an antibiotic for an infection in my eyes and to prevent infection from eye surgery. The first time after the eye drop antibiotic, I bled and most of my pain disappeared.

I figured surely I would see this Emory doctor since they have dropped the ball so many times. Well, I did not. I even call to find out if I would see this person. They person could not tell me if I would see this person. They could not tell me. What is strange I call several days ago, and the person could find if I would be seeing this doctor?

Yes, I was surprised when I walk into ENT, and they told me that I would —see Brennan again. I was nice. An intern came in to observe Brennan. I tried to tell him about the recent bleeding; he did listen. He scope me telling the intern — "He has no growths."

A week later I went to my neurologist appointment. They spend a little over an hour with me. They told me that they send a note and get another ENT appointment. What is unbelievable about this appointment — it took me over six months to see the neurologist? I did call the choice program — what a joke. No doctor wanted to deal with the Veteran Administration. Yet, a year ago when I had my pain in my head. I tried to make an eye appointment. It took four or five months for the choice to get their act together. I was so frustrated and in my pain - I was trying to find the reason for my pain. The VA personnel did not care especially in the ENT department for over thirty years I had told them the symptoms and about my pain. NOTHING WAS DONE!!!!!! Yes, I thought and said those things about ending it all. HELL NO CARE!!!!!! I knew better but still I voice my desperation. It had taken 8 hours before they came to where I was living for the police to come to check on me. If I had been really serious, I would have been dead.

I call the social worker to find if they neurologist had made my ENT appointment. She told me - "No.". I went to Stockbridge Clinic for me B-12 shot. It took five or four months to my B-12 through the mail from the VA. Another mess up. After the shot, I got my shot, I got my appointment schedule. On the print out was a ENT appointment for the 8th of September. I call when I got home I call the ENT department. This time the person could tell me who I was going to see. Guess who? Brennan, another appointment with a useless person who does not do their job or listen the patient. I told the person on the phone what had happen and I was supposed to see a 'real' doctor. Now, I have to wait only a month and half. During this time I am bleeding slowly from somewhere in my body;. When I complain about this the people tell me - go to the emergency room.

What another BIT JOKE! I have been there and experience this disastrous place both at Kaiser, at a hospital, and at the VA. This brings up that memory. Yes, I went there once. My gut was killing me. I had the runs and sinuses on the left was running like a faucet. I waited six or more hours. I was finally the next person to be seen. I could the drainage from left sinus or ear region. It was like a water coming from a spring and it stop suddenly. I told the doctor or whoever it was about this. His reply was - "This cannot be the cause of your symptoms. Well, the symptoms went away in a couple of hours. The person did not do anything for me or given anything. Another a person who did not listen or care. Was it 'PROTOCOL'?

What is really sad after all the abuse 'no is worried about me being alive and if I am better'.

I have told the Director and Bowser that should take their sign in the reception area that says-Service and help the veteran is why they are there.

Pat glanced up to see if Ted was still there. He was taken by this man words nothing could enter his thoughts. Ted was still there.

"Why don't you get another drink....It's on the house," remarked to Ted?

Focusing his eyes back on the words written on the yellow paper, Pat could hear Ted move the bamboo chair.

There was one person who went to bat for me to try to help me. He was Dr. Ponkshe. Several years he arrange an appointment with the infections disease section the VA. I went taking my empty bottle of anti-fungus meds - I had misplace the current med that I was taking at the time. They took my blood pressure it was a little low. The nurse took it again and it had drop twenty points. I went to see this doctor. I explain my history and told him that I had left my current meds at home but I had the bottle of my old meds.. He took the bottle and after our talk left the room and came back. He gave me the old bottle back and told me to continue to take this med. After he told me this he told me - "We can't help you." In other words, go to my outside provider and use them. I knew then this was a dead end. One more time the Veterans Administration couldn't care less about me being mess up. What is strange and a good thing? I have taken this new meds off and on for several years. The results was granted strange. At times, I eat and drink with my left hand. I am right handed and my choice in music has change to classical from country. I guess the brain changes when the fungus is disappearing from ones brain and body.

This past year, I was living with a woman. One day, I went home and found my belongings on the back porch. I guess she could not change me, and there was element about money in our relationship. Women do not like to go with a person who is poor.

Dr. Ponshe on one of a visit to with him call the head of Social Services to met with me. In our meeting, she told me that she would help me find a 'job' and a place to live. Well, this person directed me to Fort McPherson. After it was all over with- I had to find my own funding for housing for three months. For numerous months, I was shifted from this person to that person with nothing being done. One time, I called the Director's office and told them that I had called this woman at McPherson numerous times, and she would not return my calls - I need help finding me a place to live. I got a call in a couple of days on a Sunday. On the phone, this woman gave me a list of apartments-more than half of the telephone numbers did work, and the rest did not help anyone or had a waiting list of six months.

I tried to call the Director about this, but she did not return my calls. After two months when I was in the reception area of the Directors Office, I ask the receptionist to call this person - He responded — "She will never return your calls." Another dead end.

I am now looking for more help. I have a limited income, and my health does not permit to last long in doing anything. The Atlanta VA does not care about that. Remember what the doctor told me about my low blood pressure. — "Go back to your outside provider."

Did I mention, it took numerous months to get my B-12 meds from the VA.

The put off with finding someone to pull my bad teeth. Here is a list. Over half were bad phone numbers and do not exist. The others you have to wait three to four months. Luckily, the nerves with these teeth are nearly dead.

Pat let go of what he had read and picked up another sheet.

During the course of all this mess of trying to find relief from my pain and filing a tort or seeking help, I went to a source that I thought could do something to help me. I was totally wrong. From the Senators and Congressman, they told me this-"We don't have any power." One Congressman did get me to talk to the Director who was new at the VA in Atlanta. Her name was Williams-I think. One day, I got a call and ask to come to the VA to talk to the Director. I went. Sorry. What a Joke and waste of time. In entering the conference room there were all the department's that I had sought help from. The people missing was the ENT department. I was ask what I wanted. I replied — "I want to be well — rid of my pain." I was promised by everyone that they would achieve my goal. The assistant to the person who control the clinics was there and told me after the meeting. "My door is always open to you. Just give me a call. A month later, I woke up with the most unbelievable pain. I call this person. He said, "I have two doctors in front of me. I'll call you back." He did not!!! I call him again about a month later. I got the same response. I did not call him again. Would you?

After everyone had left, a lady took me to her office and filled out a disability claim. I told her about my eye problem and other issues. She only filed for the ringing in my ears.

Speaking for filing for disability, After the deal of me catching all the messes up that the personnel has done to me. I get a letter saying that I did not file the correct forms. The recent disability claim was denied. I never got a physical exam or anything. I follow the directions of the social worker who is in charge of my file. I was told to go to the DAV office on the hill which is next to the hospital and see this person for knew what to do with my case and file the correct forms. The question is - "Why do I get blame for filing the wrong forms?" No One wants to deal with this one either.

Once I file a 'tort'. It was denied in the Atlanta region. I file the tort to DC. Believe it or not, I could talk to the 'lawyer' who was handling my tort case. At first contact, she told that it would be nine months before there would be a decision on my tort. During the fourth or third month, I call the lawyer to tell her that I would be sending material from the hospital where the diagnosis that I had been over-dose with blood pressure meds for ten years. She responded-"We don't take outside material, but your tort has been denied. What happen to the rest of the months that were left. It doesn't take a rocket scientist — these people pile up the torts — had a person come in read them and then they could say that they looked at them.

A side note, I work with a person who works reading these things. She told him — "Most do not read them if they read them they only read a small portion of the file and then decline the file." I had a friend a Warrant Officer. He was in a plane crash while on duty. The data in his record told these people-He had an injury from this plane crash. He was denied his claim.

The stories are told of Vietnam Vets going out to the Atlanta VA trying to file a claim for agent orange and other related diseases while in Vietnam. They would be put off and put off. Why did they get the runaround? My guess, it is like my PA remark — "It was protocol." My guess it same as the ENT people not printing out a Cat Scan after time and time I went out there and had an infection after infection - "It is protocol." At the time, they wanted their bonuses for cutting cost too.

Pat stared at what he had just read. Suddenly, he let the sheets go. They fell to the floor. As he picked up another yellow sheet, he wonder how could this tale get any worse.

I suddenly remember, I mess up. Way back there, I was given a counselor to help me. Her comment was - "You're one of those that have drop between the cracks." Looking at this statement , it was half way right. She wanted me be to be disable and file for a disability. I was stupid. I told her, "I want to be well and have a regular job. Nothing was done, however.

I need to stop.

I need to drink some more to forget all the rejection, the begging and pleading for help.

I need to forget all this Hell!!

But relief came from the oddest place. I had gone to my outside provider for my eyes were hurting more than usual. The doctor informed me that I had infection. The doctor gave me some antibiotic eye drops. After I done these drops, I bled one Sunday morning from my nose. A couple days later, I realize that my pain was decreasing in my head. The doctor a couple of months later gave me the same meds to prevent infection after my first cataract surgery. I bled once more from the nose and one evening bled bright red blood from my mouth. I do not have any teeth in my upper mouth and no sores. The passage ways in my nose open up.

I tried to tell the doctors at the Atlanta VA but they would not listen or explain what was or is going in my head.

They do not want to hear from the patient. Years ago I told this to the ENT doctors. I went to get a tooth pull. The dentist took my blood pressure. It was 140. He waited twenty or so minutes and check the blood pressure again. It registered 170. While in the chair the mass came down from the left sinus area. Most of this mass hung *up in the back of throat. The doc took my blood pressure again. It had drop to 125. What is amazing the ENT doctors at the Atlanta VA would deal with this.*

I need a drink.

Before I really get drunk, I should do my ritual with my toy. I wonder if I will live.

I am exhausted mentally. I have been beaten up so bad and I have nothing. Only. one person went out his way to really help who had the power to help me.

No one in DC every call me with Veterans Administration. I guess that I am just a pile of SHIT!

Pat looked up at Ted again as he pick up last of the yellow sheets. Pat look down at the page it read.

What did I do wrong?

All wanted was to get rid of pain and be a functional human being.

Pat lean over looking directly at Ted a started to speak. "Ted! It' all about money, understaffing and a style of behavior was done for years by the Veterans Administration staff.'

There was a dead silence before Pat spoke again. "Take this right way. 'We are no-bodies. We don't have money, or you are someone knows the state or nationwide. As you read in his writing, he tried and tried and tried to get results." Pat stop speaking and began again. "I am not putting you down, but those are the facts. I have done the same thing and got the same results and known others who have been on that same path.

You need to think of your friend what he was — a good guy who wanted to be well and people did not want to help him. I've lost some friends like Fred.., Don't worry about the cost of the drinks and the moon-pie, Harry gives me a big discount," Pat stop talking as got up out of the bamboo chair. He stood by Ted for a minute while he place this left hand on his right shoulder.

Pat stood there. It seem, to him like an eternity. 'I say or do anything more for Ted. What he had tried by the government system is slower than a snail and the consequences usually is a big zero.

"Leave your phone number with Harry in the front. I have to relieve myself. We've talk for a long time, and that is fine., Pat said in a low caring voice as Ted turn and started to walk away "Remember, I am here Wednesday and Thursday afternoons. I will be for you." Pat knew that Ted would not come back. The man would get angry and probably get drunk to kill the pain; he was powerless to do anything for his friend, turning toward the facilities as Harry call them shaking his head in disgust and knowing this was not isolated incident from these people. Nothing would be done if Ted wrote his Congressman or Senator nothing would be done. It was 'Protocol' as the turkey and replied to Fred about just giving him a 1,000 aspirin. They just put you off like a horse wanting that carrot in front of him, putting roadblocks to a person getting help mentally and the physical and just surviving with your sickness.

"Where you going?" a voice rang out. It was Harry's voice.

"I am going to the 'facilities' to refreshen up," Pat responded. He wondered if he would cry. He didn't need to relieve himself. He was hurting inside. How can another human deny another human relief from their pain and agony? This wasn't decent behavior from any human being to another. Pat thought of Nancy. She had been there for him at night with those ugly years when those memories would come every night. Pat smile. He someone that cared for him. Those memories now only came once in a while every year. Poor Fred had just a neighbor that would come over just about every to check on his friend.

He had gone to the people who were supposed to help him but they only push him aside and never really did anything for him.

www.ingramcontent.com/pod-product-compliance
Lightning Source LLC
Chambersburg PA
CBHW052029280526
45793CB00005B/1176